U.S. WOMEN'S NATIONAL SOCCER TEAM

SPORTS UNITE US

Published in the United States of America by Cherry Lake Publishing
Ann Arbor, Michigan
www.cherrylakepublishing.com

Reading Adviser: Marla Conn MS, Ed., Literacy specialist, Read-Ability, Inc.

Photo Credits: ©Shaun Botterill/Getty Images, cover; ©Kevin C. Cox/Getty Images, 1; ©Jim Ruymen/ UPI/Getty Images, 5; ©Ronald Martinez/Getty Images, 6; ©Michael Loccisano/Getty Images, 9; ©Eric Thayer/Getty Images, 10; ©Jerritt Clark/Getty Images, 11; ©Kevin C. Cox/Getty Images, 15; ©Brad Smith/ISIPhotos/ZUMA Wire/Getty Images, 16; ©Patrick McDermott/Getty Images, 17; ©Brad Smith/ ISIPhotos/ZUMA Wire/Getty Images, 21; ©Jason Kempin/Getty Images, 22; ©Stephen Dunn/Getty Images, 25; ©Scott Barbour/Getty Images, 26; ©Francois Laplante/FreestylePhoto/Getty Images, 28; ©Dennis Grombkowski/Getty Images, 28; ©Dennis Grombkowski/Getty Images, 29; ©Ronald Martinez/ Getty Images, 30

Library of Congress Cataloging-in-Publication Data has been filed and is available at catalog.loc.gov

Cherry Lake Publishing would like to acknowledge the work of The Partnership for 21st Century Learning.
Please visit *www.p21.org* for more information.

Printed in the United States of America
Corporate Graphics

ABOUT THE AUTHOR

J.E. Skinner received a Bachelor of Arts in Anthropology from Wake Forest University. She loves writing both fiction and nonfiction books. In addition to reading as much as she can, when J.E. isn't writing, she is hiking with her dogs and spending time with her family in the beautiful outdoors.

TABLE OF CONTENTS

CHAPTER 1

The Game That Started a Movement

Soccer is one of the most popular sports in the world. The earliest records show a form of soccer called Tsu'Chu played in the Han dynasty in the third to fourth century. In 1863, London clubs codified the game. Soccer officially split from rugby and became its own sport.

Millions of people spanning six continents play soccer each year. Clubs, camps, and tournaments help players of all abilities practice their skills and technique. The biggest soccer tournament is the World Cup, which is played every four years. Millions of fans watched the Women's World Cup in 2015. Interest in women's soccer exploded in 1999.

The 1999 **FIFA** Women's World Cup brought country-wide and global attention to women's soccer. China

Representing the United States of America in the 1999 Women's World Cup.

and the United States played excellent **offense** and **defense**. Following the regular 90 minutes of play and 30 minutes of extra time, neither team had scored. Despite her typical brilliant performance, **forward** Mia Hamm, widely considered the best female soccer player in the world, was unable to score. With the temperature in the 90s Fahrenheit (30s Celsius), both exhausted teams chose five players to take **penalty** kicks. The ball was placed on a circle 12 yards (11 meters) from the goal. China and the U.S. took turns shooting. China missed its third penalty kick.

The Americans win the 2015 Women's World Cup.

The game ended in a thunder of cheers when U.S. defender Brandi Chastain sent the ball flying into the goal with her **nondominant** left foot.

Sixteen years later, the American women played again in the 2015 Women's World Cup Finals, this time against Japan. With 26.7 million viewers, it was the most watched soccer game in American history. Star forward Carli Lloyd scored a hat trick—three goals—during the game. Her third goal, scored with a kick from the halfway line, remains one of the most impressive goals ever scored. Lloyd is the only woman to score a hat trick in a World Cup Final. Her hat trick was the earliest in World Cup history and the fastest hat trick in Women's World Cup history.

The 1999 and 2015 Women's World Cups showed that the U.S. Women's **National** Team (USWNT) was the best team in the world. They proved that women's soccer was an elite sport and that people around the world enjoyed watching women's sports. The 1999 and 2015 squads inspired girls of all ages to play soccer, and encouraged men to support women as outstanding athletes.

Greatest Living Players

Mia Hamm is one of the greatest soccer players of all time. She was named one of FIFA's 125 greatest living players by Pelé. Pelé was a retired Brazilian forward thought to be the greatest soccer player of all time. Hamm had the highest number of international goals until 2013—more than nine years after she retired. After her brother passed away in 1997, Hamm created a foundation to help those who need bone marrow or cord blood **transplants**.

CHAPTER 2

Fighting for Their Rights

The USWNT has always fought for women's rights. They also encourage boys and girls to support each other. For years, the women have fought against playing on plastic **turf**. It has been found to be unsafe and unhealthy. Sliding on the turf can cause cuts and infections when the bits of plastic get into the wound. The turf might even cause cancer, because players inhale the plastic pieces. Also, some of the turf pieces aren't put together evenly and can cause players to trip. In December 2015, during their Women's World Cup Victory Tour, the USWNT refused to play a match because one section of the turf was several inches higher than the other parts of the field. Megan Rapinoe, 2015 World Cup champion midfielder, actually peeled it up with her

New York City throws a ticker tape parade for the 2015 World Cup champions.

bare hands! The women argued that if men only play on grass, then women should, too. Despite some games played on grass, the women continue their battle to play all of their matches on grass.

Female players around the world fight for equal pay with men. In March 2016, the USWNT sued the U.S. Soccer Federation and demanded equal pay, equal playing conditions, and the same quality equipment as the men. The USWNT received some of their requests, but they still weren't paid the same. For their 2015 World Cup championship win, the squad made $2 million in

Democratic presidential candidate and former Secretary of State Hillary Clinton speaks with midfielder Megan Rapinoe.

prize money. To compare, the 2014 men's world champions, Germany, won $35 million in prize money. Many men and women support the team's fight for equal pay. Landon Donovan, a forward and attacking midfielder for the U.S. men's team, **tweeted** that the "#USWNT absolutely deserve to be treated fairly in all ways."

After the 1999 World Cup championship, floods of girls joined soccer leagues. The USWNT continues to encourage girls of all ages to feel proud and strong. The efforts of the U.S. women's

Former midfielder Julie Foudy speaks about the importance of sports for kids.

team inspire other countries to recognize that women's sports are as popular as men's. One way they do this is through the Empowering Women and Girls through Sports **initiative**. Since boys accept girls playing sports more than they used to, the USWNT can teach **clinics** to boys and girls at the same time. USWNT players travel the world holding soccer clinics for youth who can't usually find places to play. They train young boys and girls on techniques and methods. They also teach boys and girls about the importance of acceptance, leadership, and **diversity**.

Recognition

Due to the USWNT's efforts, more women are being represented in sports. In 2015, Sports Illustrated named tennis player Serena Williams Sportsperson of the Year. Also, the Women's Sports Foundation recognizes women in sports. The Billie Jean King Contribution Award, named after the winner of the 1973 "Battles of the Sexes" tennis match, supports women who have shown they are strong leaders. The Yolanda L. Jackson Give Back Award rewards women who are brave role models and who give back to their communities.

Julie Foudy

Julie Foudy was a Stanford University graduate who played midfield for the 1999 Women's World Cup team. She was the captain of the USWNT from 2000 until 2004. After she retired from soccer, Foudy joined the broadcasting world and announced many women's games. In addition, she commented on and analyzed many matches, including the Women's World Cup and the UEFA Euro 2008. Foudy continues to be an **advocate** for girls to learn self-confidence. She also wants women to find their voice and fight for their rights. Foudy played a major role in preventing any changes to the federal law Title IX. She also won the FIFA Fair Play Award. This award celebrates fair play and compassion in sports. Foudy spoke out against sweatshops in the making of soccer equipment.

CHAPTER 3

To Reach Out a Hand

The USWNT makes a real effort to connect with its fans. There is a page on the women's U.S. Soccer Federation website called "One Nation. One Team. 23 stories." There, the 2015 Women's World Cup players share funny and thoughtful videos about themselves. In one video, 2011 and 2015 World Cup medalist Tobin Heath, a midfielder, tells about how she travels often and meets all kinds of interesting people. Kelley O'Hara, a wingback and medalist in the 2011 and 2015 World Cups, shares that visiting different countries as a teenager "really opened my eyes to what else was out there." Many of the players talk about playing sports when they were younger. Most say they were passionate about soccer from an early age.

American fans cheer for their team during the 2015 Women's World Cup.

In September 2017, Megan Rapinoe and forward Alex Morgan joined the Common Goal initiative. Juan Mata of the men's soccer team Manchester United had an idea to "help fund **grassroots** charities that use [soccer] to strengthen communities." His goal is to get as many players as possible to donate one percent of their income. The members of the group realize that soccer can strengthen a community. The money from the group can be used to build fields, buy uniforms, and hire coaches for new teams. Rapinoe joined the group because she

A young fan gets a jersey autographed by the U.S. Women's Team during a 2017 training session.

thought it was important for women to be involved. She thought women should support each other and set good examples for boys and girls.

In 2016 and 2017, Morgan and her teammates granted wishes for the Make-A-Wish Foundation. This nonprofit group helps people with life-threatening illnesses fulfill a wish from their wishlist. The group makes the wish come true. Several soccer fans were able to meet the players. One girl met and

France wins the 2017 SheBelieves Cup.

passed a soccer ball with Morgan. Afterwards, Morgan gave her a signed jersey. The USWNT always thanks the fans from the Make-A-Wish Foundation for their bravery and their strength. The women's team believes their supporters inspire them to always fight, no matter how hard the battle may seem.

The SheBelieves Cup occurs in the United States between teams from four countries. In 2017, Germany, France, England, and the U.S. took part. The USWNT donated the proceeds from the tournament to the SheBelieves organization. This group inspires all girls to "be strong, smart, and bold." The goal is to teach girls and women they can create success if they work hard and believe in themselves. SheBelieves shows girls the importance of teamwork and a good attitude.

Teaching Young Leaders

Sports **Envoys** *are players from the men's and women's national teams who travel to different countries. They hold soccer clinics and camps to teach girls valuable lessons in skills, techniques, confidence, and self-esteem. The programs also help form girls' teams and talk about ways to bring more attention to girls' sports. The envoys teach girls and boys about being good leaders. They also talk about the importance of diversity and of treating others with respect.*

Title IX

Title IX is a federal law that does not allow **discrimination** based on gender in higher education. Activist groups also use Title IX to support women in the workplace. It has been used to tackle inequality against women wherever it has existed. The spirit of the law has often been used in women's sports. One of the first instances was the "Battles of the Sexes" in 1973, when Billie Jean King defeated Bobby Riggs. She demanded equal pay for female tennis players. In 2016, the USWNT sued the U.S. Soccer Federation for pay equal to the men. The USWNT also fought for first-class airline seats, since the men always traveled first-class. Julie Foudy fought to prevent any changes to the law in order to protect and empower women.

CHAPTER 4

A Melting Pot

Many people come to the United States because they believe they will lead a more successful life there. The United States is called a "melting pot" because there is a lot of diversity in the country. Some people wonder why there isn't more diversity on the USWNT. Critics believe that talent exists in many places and shouldn't depend on the color of one's skin. The USWNT heard these ideas and took them to heart.

During a training session in January 2017, coach Jill Ellis called up 35 players. Of those players, 11 were African American. Ellis said, "Our youth national teams and colleges are more diverse than they have ever been. It's then natural that our senior team be reflective of this positive growth." A growing number of diverse youths are joining high school and college soccer teams

Sofia Huerta looks for the ball during a game against New Zealand in 2017.

and will soon try out for the national team. Amy Rodriguez, a Cuban American forward, has played on the USWNT since 2011. Sofia Huerta is a Mexican American defender who officially plays for the United States at the international level.

In addition to racial diversity, the USWNT supports members of the **LGBTQ** community. Former forward Abby Wambach and midfielder Megan Rapinoe have openly come out as gay, as has coach Jill Ellis. Many players worried their career would end if they revealed they were gay. These players were willing to take the

Former player Lori Lindsay attends a gala in 2011 dedicated to women in sports.

risk to help youths know that there was support for them. Lori Lindsay, a former midfielder for the women's team, said she wanted to be "a role model [for] young kids/teenagers who are struggling with their sexuality or afraid to come out." Given that there are no openly gay male soccer players, the USWNT wants to support boys and girls struggling with their sexuality.

In the United States, there are many competitive leagues. The leagues require fees and are called "pay-to-play" soccer. Poorer families may not be able to afford uniforms or travel for games.

There are some ideas about how to fix this problem. It's possible for richer parents to help pay for families that don't have much money. Another idea is to limit how often competitive teams play. Not playing in the league year-round would help players take a mental and physical break. They could play **pickup** games with their friends and communities. Pickup games could make soccer more fun for players and would allow more people to play and learn new skills.

Women of Color

Until 2015, the USWNT was largely **Caucasian**. *There weren't many role models for women of color. Sydney Leroux, Shannon Boxx, and Christen Press changed that. Lynn Williams, a newer forward for the team, remembers watching soccer but feeling like "you didn't really see a lot of women of color on TV." Starting in 2016, young girls of color were able to watch several African American women playing with the best soccer team in the world.*

CHAPTER 5

The Legacy

The USWNT quietly won the 1991 Women's World Cup. The players worked out and kept practicing. They won a gold medal at the 1996 Olympics. Americans slowly became interested in the sport. Organizers for the 1999 World Cup focused on girls' youth clubs and teams. They worked on igniting interest at younger ages. Organizers hoped to spark national interest in a sport that had mostly been ignored. It worked.

The 1999 World Cup was hugely popular. It put women's soccer in the spotlight. Girls flooded onto teams and joined their high school, club, and college teams. The 1999 team spent a fair amount of time encouraging girls to play and to "dare to dream." Several players set up camps to teach girls good technique. They also taught girls the importance of working together. They

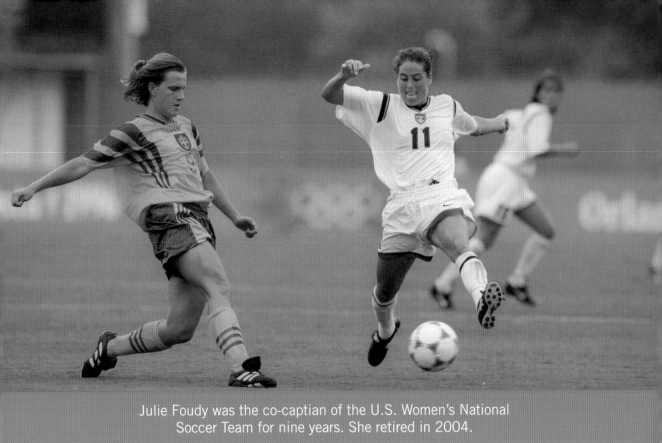
Julie Foudy was the co-captian of the U.S. Women's National Soccer Team for nine years. She retired in 2004.

wanted youths to build each other up, not tear each other down.

The popularity of soccer and the USWNT spread to other countries. Australia, Canada, and Europe all strengthened their teams. Naturally, this drew the attention of the male-run U.S. Soccer Federation and FIFA. Women's soccer dominates American soccer. The USWNT are the reigning international champions with three World Cup trophies. They have won four of the past five Olympic gold medals and have been ranked no lower than second in the international charts.

Goalkeeper Briana Scurry stops a goal during practice.

The USWNT encourages communities to provide safe spaces for girls and boys. These spaces allow youths to feel safe no matter what color their skin is. The USWNT wants LGBTQ youths to feel no shame in being themselves. Openly gay players and coaches advocate for youths. They hope to be role models for those questioning their sexuality. The USWNT works with many **outreach** programs. These programs provide a sense of community for youths.

The USWNT team took a women's sport that held little interest and turned it into a sport that men and women watch

[21ST CENTURY SKILLS LIBRARY]

worldwide. The players have proven time and again that they are a force, not just a team. The players advocate for girls to strive for what they want to achieve. The USWNT teaches girls and boys how to work hard and to feel proud of their accomplishments. They teach girls and boys how to problem-solve. Most importantly, the USWNT teaches youths how to overcome struggles and to succeed in all aspects of their lives.

A Role Model for All

Briana Scurry was the goalkeeper for the 1999 Women's World Cup. She was named Player of the Match for her save against Liu Ying. Scurry dove left, punching the ball away. Scurry was the only African American on the team. She was also gay, but not openly, since sports in the 1990s were not as tolerant toward homosexuality. She inspired women of color to be proud and achieve their dreams, regardless of the color of their skin or their sexuality.

1996
The USWNT wins their first Olympic gold medal.

1991
The USWNT wins their first Women's World Cup.

1990

1999
The team wins the World Cup again, which launches women's soccer both nationally and internationally.

2015

The U.S. becomes the only team to win three World Cups. Carli Lloyd scores a hat trick in the final against Japan. The team is awarded a ticker-tape parade in New York City and meets President Barack Obama in the White House.

2017

The USWNT donates proceeds from the 2017 SheBelieves Cup to Girls, Inc.

2010

2012

The U.S. wins the gold medal for the fourth time at the Olympics. The National Women's Soccer League is formed to provide opportunities for fringe players.

2015

The team sues the U.S. Soccer Federation to play on grass instead of turf. In a compromise, the team plays some, but not all games, on grass. Megan Rapinoe gets an ACL injury from uneven turf, and the team refuses to play a game in Hawaii for their 2015 World Cup Victory Tour.

Look closely at this photo. Can you see the camaraderie amongst the teammates? Why is it important for a team to work well together?

Why is a women's soccer league important to girls and to women? What can it teach men about the value of women's sports?

Can you imagine yourself winning a World Cup? What steps would you take to get there?

Learn More

BOOKS

Alexander, Heather. *U.S. Women's Soccer: Go for Gold!* New York: Penguin Young Readers, 2016.

Downing, Erin. *For Soccer-Crazy Girls Only.* New York: Feiwel & Friends, 2014.

Morgan, Alex. *Breakaway: Beyond the Goal.* New York: Simon & Schuster BFYR, 2015.

ON THE WEB

Common Goal Initiative
https://www.common-goal.org

Global Sports Envoys
https://globalsportsmentoring.org

USWNT Official Website
https://www.ussoccer.com/womens-national-team#tab-1

GLOSSARY

advocate (AD-vuh-kit) one who supports or promotes the interests of a cause or group; to plead for or on behalf of another

Caucasian (kah-KAY-zhun) the racial group commonly referred to as white

clinics (KLIH-niks) group meetings for teaching certain skills and techniques

defense (DEE-fence) protecting one's own goal

discrimination (dih-skrih-mih-NAY-shin) unfair treatment of a person, racial group, or minority based on prejudice

diversity (dih-VUR-sih-tee) having individuals from different genders, races, faiths, or cultures within one group of people

envoys (AHN-voyz) representatives for a cause or group

FIFA (FEE-FUH) an abbreviation for the Fédération Internationale de Football Association; the international governing body of soccer

forward (FOHR-wurd) a player who is responsible for most of a team's scoring and who plays closest to the opponent's goal

grassroots (GRAS-roots) common people who bring awareness to or start an organization or idea

initiative (ih-NISH-uh-tiv) a new plan or process to achieve something or solve a problem

LGBTQ (ELL JEE BEE TEE CUE) an abbreviation for lesbian, gay, bisexual, and transgender

national (NASH-uh-nul) belonging to a nation

nondominant (nahn-DAH-mih-nent) the least-used or least-developed of a pair of body parts, such as hands, eyes, or feet

offense (AH-fence) attacking or moving toward the opponent's goal

outreach (OWT-reech) the extending of services or assistance beyond usual limits

penalty (PEN-uhl-tee) a consequence caused by the violation of a law or rule

pickup (PIK-up) an unofficial game that has been spontaneously started by a group of players

transplants (TRANS-plants) an operation in which an organ or tissue is moved from one person to another

turf (TURF) a substitute for grass made from artificial fibers

tweet (TWEET) to make a post on the social media platform Twitter

INDEX